AF270830

Small child

once you were a hope, a dream.
Now you are reality.
Changing all that is to come.
So small. A flick of star stuff.
A mind to touch the edges of the universe.
A love to hold our hearts forever.

CHARLOTTE GRAY

Welcome, Baby!

PLACE PHOTO HERE

Before You Were Born

Before you were conceived I wanted you.
Before you were born I loved you…
This is the miracle of life.
MAUREEN HAWKINS

When your parents met, we _____

_____

_____

_____

_____

_____

_____

_____

_____

_____

Why having you felt important to us _____

_____

_____

_____

_____

_____

A new baby is like the beginning of all things—
wonder, hope, a dream of possibilities.

EDA LeSHAN

Great Expectations

On the day we found out you were coming, we _____

_____

_____

_____

_____

_____

_____

How we knew you were on the way _____

_____

_____

_____

_____

_____

_____

Who we told first _____

_____

_____

_____

_____

_____

_____

_____

How we celebrated _____

_____

_____

_____

_____

_____

_____

Showered with Love

Shared joy is double joy…
SWEDISH PROVERB

The first party for you was _____

_____

_____

_____

_____

_____

_____

It was held on _____

_____

_____

And was hosted by _____

_____

_____

The most surprising gift was _____

_____

_____

The best piece of advice we received was _____

_____

_____

_____

Counting the Days

A mother's joy begins when new life is stirring inside,
when a tiny heartbeat is heard for the very first time,
and a playful kick reminds her that she is never alone.

UNKNOWN

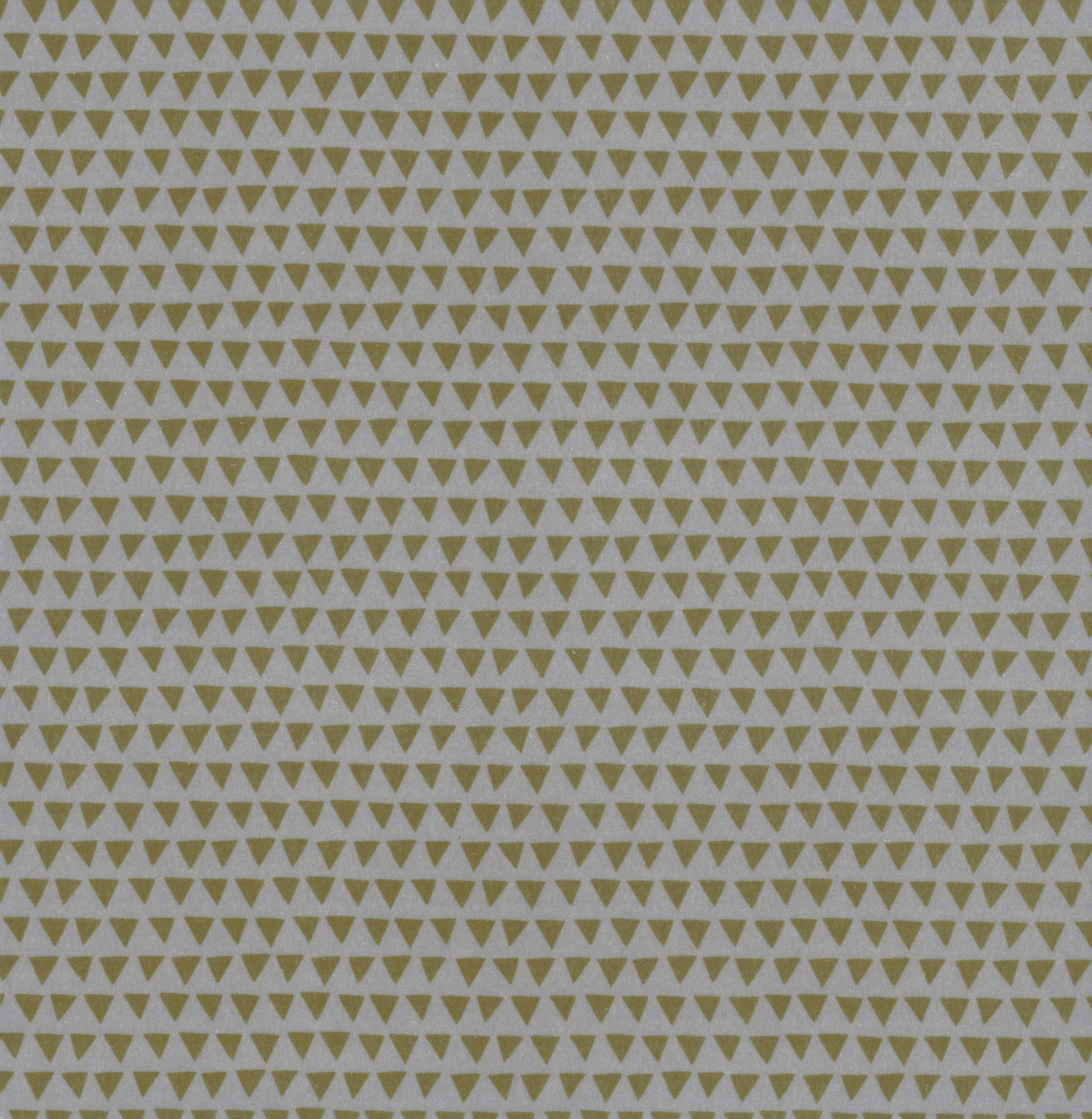

PLACE SONOGRAM HERE

Waiting for you was _____

_____

_____

_____

We expected you to come on _____

_____

There is nothing on earth like that moment of seeing one's first baby.
KATHARINE TREVELYAN

The Day You Were Born

Seeing you for the first time was _____

_____

_____

_____

_____

_____

_____

_____

_____

_____

_____

_____

_____

_____

_____

You were born on _____ *at* _____ *in the city of* _____

You weighed _____ *and measured* _____

Welcome to the World

"Where have I come from, where did you pick me up?"
the baby asked its mother.
She answered, half crying, half laughing,
and clasping the baby to her breast,——
"You were hidden in my heart as its
desire, my darling.
You were in the dolls of my
childhood's games…
In all my hopes and my loves,
in my life, in the life of my mother
you have lived."

RABINDRANATH TAGORE

The Story of Your Birth Day

Mom's Story

No one understands how someone so little can so change their world—
until they hold their baby in their arms.

PAM BROWN

Dad's Story

All Your Visitors

...what joy is welcomed like a new-born child?

CAROLINE NORTON

Another Name for Love

When you name your baby,
it's a time of dreaming.

LAURA WATTENBERG

We chose your name because _____

_____

_____

_____

_____

_____

_____

_____

We considered naming you _____

_____

_____

Nicknames we have for you _____

_____

_____

_____

_____

_____

Your Little Hands & Feet

Baby's Footprints

Such tiny hands to hold our hearts forever.

PAM BROWN

Our babies will create a world we cannot imagine,
they will accomplish things we cannot even dream.

KATHRYN T. SHAW

The World Awaits You

THE WORLD WHEN YOU WERE BORN

President's name _____

_____

Big items in the news _____

_____

_____

_____

Latest inventions _____

_____

_____

_____

Our favorite songs and TV shows _____

_____

_____

Price of a

STAMP

$ ....

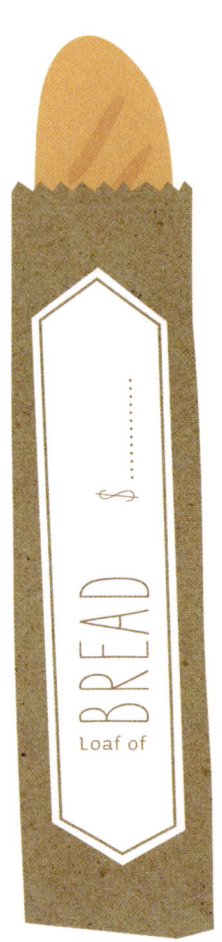

Loaf of

BREAD $ ....

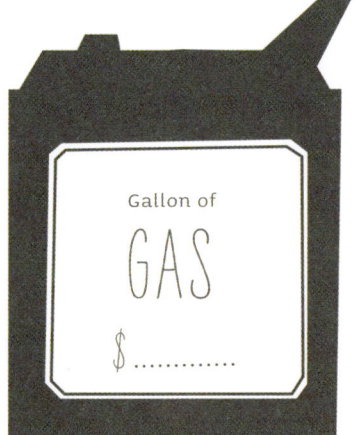

Gallon of

GAS

$ ....

MOVIE $ ....

ADMIT ONE

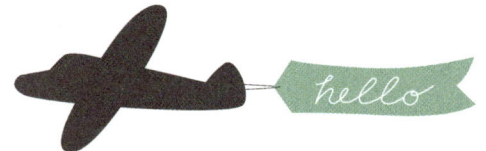

Welcome Home

Your first day home was _____

_____

_____

_____

_____

_____

_____

The weather that day _____

_____

_____

We dressed you in _____

_____

_____

Baby is here——
time to tell the world!
GERALDINE FERRARE

Some of your first visitors were _____

_____

_____

_____

_____

_____

We were very surprised by _____

_____

_____

_____

_____

Your First Room

*Family…where life begins
and love never ends.*

UNKNOWN

We wanted your room to be _____

_____

_____

_____

We chose these colors _____

_____

_____

_____

And collected books like _____

_____

_____

_____

Some of your favorite toys _____

_____

_____

_____

Some special touches _____

_____

_____

Children are a handful sometimes,
a heart-full all the time.
UNKNOWN

Getting to Know You

YOUR FIRST TWO WEEKS

A day with you is _____

_____

_____

_____

You wake up _____

_____

_____

_____

You're very active when _____

_____

_____

_____

You seem to like it when _____

_____

_____

_____

Most amazing or memorable moment _____

_____

_____

_____

_____

You've grown _____ inches and gained _____ pounds.

Our Family Tree

There are only two lasting bequests
we can hope to give our children.
One of these is roots; the other, wings.

HODDING CARTER

Great Grandma

Great Grandma

Great Grandpa

Great Grandpa

Grandpa

Grandpa

Grandma

Grandma

Brothers + Sisters

Dad

Mom

You

A brand new dream, a brand new world.

Oh, baby…Come closer. Eye to eye, soul to soul.
Come say hello to your new-born mother.

PHYLLIS CHESLER

But never a little one comes to earth that isn't a wonderful babe at birth, and never a mother who doesn't see glorious visions of joy to be.

EDGAR GUEST

Dear Child,

A letter from Mom

All that is worth cherishing begins in the heart…
SUZANNE CHAPIN

Dear Child,

A letter from Dad

Watching You Grow

THE FIRSTS, THE LASTS,
THE LITTLE MIRACLES

The baby has learned to smile,
and her smiles burst forth
like holiday sparklers,
lighting our hearts.
Joy fills the room.
At what are we smiling?
We don't know and we don't care.
We are communicating with
one another in happiness,
and the smiles are the outward display
of our delight and our love.

JOAN LOWERY NIXON

WATCHING YOU GROW

Smiles & Giggles

"I love you, little one," he whispered. And the
baby smiled for the very first time and seemed
to understand what his father had just said.

DAN ZADRA

The first time you smiled _____

_____

_____

_____

_____

_____

And the first time you laughed _____

_____

_____

_____

_____

_____

Some things that always make you smile and giggle are ___

_____

_____

_____

_____

_____

WATCHING YOU GROW

Your First Haircut

*Memories, important yesterdays,
were once todays. Treasure and notice today.*

GLORIA GAITHER

A Lock of Your Hair

Watching you get your first haircut was _____

_____

_____

_____

Your first haircut was on _____

And we went to _____

_____

_____

Watching You Grow

Lullabies & Good Nights

I can still remember rocking them to sleep on my lap in the middle of the night, to soothe them back to sleep after a stomach ache or a bad dream, the songs I would make up...

BETTY FRIEDAN

Some of the songs we sing to you are _____

_____

_____

These things that make you happy and sleepy _____

_____

_____

_____

_____

Our bedtime routine is _____

_____

_____

_____

_____

_____

WATCHING YOU GROW

First & Second

Months

Every child begins the world again...

HENRY DAVID THOREAU

You're changing _____

_____

_____

_____

_____

And now you can _____

_____

_____

_____

_____

You like _____

_____

_____

_____

_____

And I'll never forget _____

_____

_____

_____

_____

_____

_____

You've grown _____ inches and gained _____ pounds.

WATCHING YOU GROW

Third & Fourth

Months

Babies touch the world with love.
UNKNOWN

You're changing _____

_____

_____

_____

_____

And now you can _____

_____

_____

_____

_____

You like _____

_____

_____

_____

And I'll never forget _____

_____

_____

_____

_____

_____

You've grown _____ inches and gained _____ pounds.

WATCHING YOU GROW

Fifth & Sixth

Months

The simplest toy, one which even the youngest
child can operate, is called a grandparent.

SAM LEVENSON

You're changing _____

_____

_____

_____

_____

And now you can _____

_____

_____

_____

_____

_____

You like _____

_____

_____

_____

_____

And I'll never forget _____

_____

_____

_____

_____

_____

_____

_____

You've grown _____ *inches and gained* _____ *pounds.*

WATCHING YOU GROW

Seventh & Eighth
Months

*I actually remember feeling delight, at two o'clock in the morning,
when the baby woke for his feed, because I so longed to have another look at him.*

MARGARET DRABBLE

You're changing _____

_____

_____

_____

And now you can _____

_____

_____

_____

You like _____

_____

_____

_____

And I'll never forget _____

_____

_____

_____

_____

_____

You've grown _____ inches and gained _____ pounds.

WATCHING YOU GROW

Ninth & Tenth Months

Children reinvent your world for you.
SUSAN SARANDON

You're changing _____

_____

_____

_____

_____

And now you can _____

_____

_____

_____

_____

You like _____

_____

_____

_____

And I'll never forget _____

_____

_____

_____

_____

_____

You've grown _____ *inches and gained* _____ *pounds.*

WATCHING YOU GROW

Eleventh & Twelfth
Months

Dear child, I will care for you, protect you—until you are grown.
And then I will let you fly free. But, loving you? That is for always.

CHARLOTTE GRAY

You're changing _____

_____

_____

_____

_____

And now you can _____

_____

_____

_____

_____

You like _____

_____

_____

_____

And I'll never forget _____

_____

_____

_____

_____

_____

_____

You've grown _____ inches and gained _____ pounds.

Your First Birthday

...you shall see wonders.
WILLIAM SHAKESPEARE

We celebrated your first birthday by _____

_____

_____

_____

_____

_____

_____

You wore _____

_____

_____

You received well-wishes on your special day from _____

_____

_____

_____

_____

_____

Little You

We love watching you _____
_____
_____
_____
_____
_____
_____
_____

You seem fascinated by _____
_____
_____
_____
_____
_____
_____

Think … of the world you carry within you.
RAINER MARIA RILKE

Some of your favorite things are _____

_____

_____

_____

_____

_____

_____

_____

_____

And the people you're happy to see are _____

_____

_____

_____

_____

_____

_____

A baby will make love stronger,
days shorter, nights longer,
bankroll smaller, home happier,
clothes shabbier, the past forgotten,
and the future worth living for.

UNKNOWN

Your arrival has meant some big changes for us _____

_____

_____

_____

_____

_____

_____

_____

_____

_____

_____

_____

_____

_____

_____

_____

_____

Making the decision to have a child is **momentous**. *It is to decide forever to have your* **heart** *go walking around outside your body.*

ELIZABETH STONE

...a handful of happiness, a heart full of love.

HELEN STEINER RICE

In your first year, we've started some new traditions _____

_____

_____

_____

_____

_____

And shared special moments together, like _____

_____

_____

_____

_____

Some of our hopes for the year to come include _____

_____

_____

_____

_____

_____

With special thanks to the entire Compendium family.

CREDITS:

Written and Compiled by: Dan Zadra

Edited by: M. H. Clark and Robin Lofstrom

Designed and Illustrated by: Heidi Rodriguez

Creative Direction by: Sarah Forster

© 2012 by Compendium, Inc. All rights reserved. No part of this publication may be reproduced or transmitted in any form or by any means, electronic or mechanical, including photocopy, recording, or any storage and retrieval system now known or to be invented without written permission from the publisher. Contact: Compendium, Inc., 2100 North Pacific Street, Seattle, WA 98103. *Welcome, Baby!*; Compendium; live inspired; and the format, design, layout, and coloring used in this book are trademarks and/or trade dress of Compendium, Inc. This book may be ordered directly from the publisher, but please try your local bookstore first. Call us at 800.91.IDEAS, or come see our full line of inspiring products at live-inspired.com

4th printing. Printed in China with soy inks.

COMPENDIUM®
live inspired.

In your first year, we've started some new traditions _____

_____

_____

_____

_____

_____

_____

And shared special moments together, like _____

_____

_____

_____

_____

Some of our hopes for the year to come include _____

_____

_____

_____

_____

_____

_____

With special thanks to the entire Compendium family.

CREDITS:

Written and Compiled by: Dan Zadra

Edited by: M. H. Clark and Robin Lofstrom

Designed and Illustrated by: Heidi Rodriguez

Creative Direction by: Sarah Forster

© 2012 by Compendium, Inc. All rights reserved. No part of this publication may be reproduced or transmitted in any form or by any means, electronic or mechanical, including photocopy, recording, or any storage and retrieval system now known or to be invented without written permission from the publisher. Contact: Compendium, Inc., 2100 North Pacific Street, Seattle, WA 98103. *Welcome, Baby!*; Compendium; live inspired; and the format, design, layout, and coloring used in this book are trademarks and/or trade dress of Compendium, Inc. This book may be ordered directly from the publisher, but please try your local bookstore first. Call us at 800.91.IDEAS, or come see our full line of inspiring products at live-inspired.com

4th printing. Printed in China with soy inks.

COMPENDIUM
live inspired.

...a handful of happiness, a heart full of love.

HELEN STEINER RICE